A Month with
St Teresa of Avila

Edited by Rima Devereaux

First published in Great Britain in 2018

Society for Promoting Christian Knowledge
36 Causton Street
London SW1P 4ST
www.spck.org.uk

British Library Cataloguing-in-Publication Data
A catalogue record for this book is available from the British Library

ISBN 978-0-281-07904-9
eBook ISBN 978-0-281-07905-6

Typeset by Fakenham Prepress Solutions, Fakenham, Norfolk NR21 8NN
Manufacture managed by Jellyfish
First printed in Great Britain by CPI
Subsequently digitally printed in Great Britain

eBook by Fakenham Prepress Solutions, Fakenham, Norfolk NR21 8NN

Produced on paper from sustainable forests

Introduction

St Teresa of Avila (1515–82) was the founder of the Discalced Carmelite Order and a prolific spiritual writer. Born in Avila, Spain, only a few years after Columbus's discovery of the New World and just before Luther's launch of the Protestant Reformation, she entered the Carmelite convent of the Incarnation in Avila as a young woman. She struggled with ill health but eventually felt called to found a new convent that would mark a return to the primitive Carmelite *Rule* followed by the hermits on Mount Carmel in the Middle Ages. She devoted the rest of her life to founding further convents and collaborated with the mystic St John of the Cross on the foundation of monasteries of friars.

These extracts are taken from her four major works and highlight the core concerns of her spirituality. They include her focus on prayer as friendship with God, her comparison of stages in the spiritual life to four ways of watering a garden, her pithy remarks on the Lord's Prayer (the Our Father) and her practical advice on developing the virtues needed for a life of prayer.

Teresa was a passionate woman whose forceful personality and sense of humour emerge from her writings: 'Visitors to Carmelite monasteries today continue to be startled by the down-to-earthness, naturalness, gaiety and spontaneity that they find there. It is the Carmelites' inheritance from this rich and womanly Mother.'[1] Amid the challenges and complexities of the era in which she lived and her own busy life, she retained a sense of what it means to follow Jesus:

> Understanding her as the kind of theologian she was means understanding what it meant to her to be a 'contemplative', which, as she saw it, was essentially a matter of the sustained awareness of living within the movement of God's love into creation through the life and death of Jesus Christ.[2]

Her attractive approach to the spiritual life means that she continues to defy categorization and to speak to us in the twenty-first century.

A Month with
St Teresa of Avila

DAY 1

Morning

Everything in religion was a delight to me; and it is true that now and then I used to sweep the house during those hours of the day which I had formerly spent on my amusements and my dress; and, calling to mind that I was delivered from such follies, I was filled with a new joy that surprised me, nor could I understand whence it came.

Whenever I remember this, there is nothing in the world, however hard it may be, that, if it were proposed to me, I would not undertake without any hesitation whatsoever; for I know now, by experience in many things, that if from the first I resolutely persevere in my purpose, even in this life His Majesty rewards it in a way which he only understands who has tried it.

Evening

So, then, going on from pastime to pastime, from vanity to vanity, from one occasion of sin to another, I began to expose myself exceedingly to the very greatest dangers: my soul was so distracted by many vanities that I was ashamed to draw near to God in an act of such special friendship as that of prayer. As my sins multiplied, I began to lose the pleasure and comfort I had in virtuous things: and that loss contributed to the abandonment of prayer. I see now most clearly, O my Lord, that this comfort departed from me because I had departed from you.

DAY

2

Morning

Let him not regard certain kinds of humility which exist, and of which I mean to speak. Some think it humility not to believe that God is bestowing his gifts upon them. Let us clearly understand this, and that it is perfectly clear God bestows his gifts without any merit whatever on our part; and let us be grateful to His Majesty for them; for if we do not recognize the gifts received at his hands, we shall never be moved to love him. It is a most certain truth, that the richer we see ourselves to be, confessing at the same time our poverty, the greater will be our progress, and the more real our humility.

Evening

A beginner must look upon himself as making a garden, wherein our Lord may take his delight, but in a soil unfruitful and abounding in weeds. His Majesty roots up the weeds and has to plant good herbs. Let us, then, take for granted that this is already done when a soul is determined to give itself to prayer, and has begun the practice of it. We have, then, as good gardeners, by the help of God, to see that the plants grow, to water them carefully, that they may not die but produce blossoms, which shall send forth much fragrance, refreshing to our Lord, so that he may come often for his pleasure into this garden, and delight himself in the midst of these virtues.

DAY
3

Morning

Of those who are beginners in prayer, we may say that they are those who draw the water up out of the well – a process which, as I have said, is very laborious; for they must be wearied in keeping the senses recollected, and this is a great labour, because the senses have been hitherto accustomed to distractions. It is necessary for beginners to accustom themselves to disregard what they hear or see, and to put it away from them during the time of prayer; they must be alone, and in withdrawal think over their past life . . . They must strive to meditate on the life of Christ.

Evening

His Majesty seeks and loves courageous souls; but they must be humble in their ways and have no confidence in themselves. I never saw one of those lag behind on the road; and never a cowardly soul, though aided by humility, make that progress in many years that the former makes in a few. I am astonished at the great things done on this road by encouraging oneself to undertake great things, though we may not have the strength for them at once; the soul takes a flight upwards and ascends high, though, like a little bird whose wings are weak, it grows weary and rests.

DAY

4

Morning

Let us now speak of the second manner of drawing the water . . . of the mechanism of wheel and buckets whereby the gardener may draw more water with less labour . . . I apply it to the prayer called the prayer of quiet . . .

This is a gathering together of the faculties of the soul within itself, in order that it may have the fruition of that contentment in greater sweetness; but the faculties are not lost, neither are they asleep; the will alone is occupied in such a way that, without knowing how it has become a captive, it gives a simple consent to become the prisoner of God.

Evening

Therefore, for the love of our Lord, I implore those souls to whom His Majesty has given so great a grace – the attainment of this state – to know and make much of themselves, with a humble and holy presumption, in order that they may never return to the fleshpots of Egypt . . . What I earnestly advise is this: let there be no giving up of prayer; it is by prayer they will understand what they are doing, and obtain from our Lord the grace to repent and strength to rise again; they must believe and believe again that, if they cease from praying, they run – so I think – into danger.

DAY

5

Morning

Let us now speak of the third water by which this garden is watered – water running from a river or from a brook – whereby the garden is watered with very much less trouble, although there is some in directing the water. In this state our Lord will help the gardener, and in such a way as to be, as it were, the Gardener himself, doing all the work. [This prayer] is a sleep of the powers of the soul, which are not wholly lost nor yet understanding how they function. The pleasure, sweetness and delight are incomparably greater than in the former state of prayer; and the reason is that the waters of grace have risen up to the neck of the soul, so that it can neither advance nor retreat – nor does it know how to do so; it seeks only the fruition of very great bliss.

Evening

Let us now come to what the soul feels interiorly. Let those who know how to speak of it describe it, for it is impossible to understand it and much more so to describe it. When I prepared to write this, I had just communicated, and had risen from the very prayer of which I am speaking. I am thinking of what the soul was then doing. Our Lord said to me: it undoes itself utterly, my daughter, in order that it may give itself more and more to me; it is not itself that then lives, it is I. As it cannot comprehend what it understands, it understands by not understanding.

DAY

6

Morning

Our Lord is he by whom all good things come to us; he will teach you. Consider his life; that is the best example. What more can we want than so good a friend at our side, one who will not forsake us when we are in trouble and distress, unlike those who belong to the world! Blessed are they who truly love him, and who always have him near them! Let us consider the glorious St Paul, for whom it seems Jesus was never absent from his lips, as if he had him deep down in his heart. After I had heard this about some of the great saints given to contemplation, I considered the matter carefully and understood that they followed no other path.

Evening

This father . . . was, however, very prudent and very gentle . . . for my soul was not at all strong, but rather very weak, especially in giving up certain friendships, though I did not offend God by them: there was much natural affection in them, and I thought it would be an act of ingratitude if I broke them off . . . I asked him if I must be ungrateful. He told me to lay the matter before God for a few days . . . that God might enlighten me as to the better course . . .

From that day onwards, I have had enough courage to leave all things for God, who in one moment . . . was pleased to transform his servant into another person.

DAY

7

Morning

I contrived that one of my sisters . . . should buy a house . . . with money that our Lord provided for us . . . In holding the money, in finding the house, in negotiating for it, in putting it in order, I had so much to suffer; and, for the most part, I had to suffer alone . . . Sometimes, in my affliction, I used to say: O my Lord, how is it that you command me to do what seems impossible? . . .

Once, when I was in one of my difficulties, not knowing what to do, unable to pay the workmen, St Joseph, my true father and lord, appeared to me, and gave me to understand that money would not be wanting and I must hire the workmen.

Evening

In the extremity of my trouble, our Lord said to me: 'Do you not know that I am the Almighty? What are you afraid of?' He made me feel assured that the monastery would not be broken up, and I was greatly comforted . . .

I took myself to God and said, 'O Lord, this house is not mine; it was founded for you; and now that there is no one to take up the cause, I ask you to protect it.' I now felt myself at peace, and as free from anxiety as if the whole world were on my side in the matter; and at once I looked upon it as safe.

DAY

8

Morning

What amazes me most is this: however much I may wish to pray for those graces which our Lord sees not to be expedient, I cannot do it; and if I try, I do so with little earnestness, force and spirit: it is impossible to do more, even if I would. But it is not so as to those which His Majesty intends to grant. These I can pray for constantly, and with great persistence; though I do not carry them in my memory, they seem to present themselves to me at once . . .

    The prayer that is not to be heard is, so to speak, like vocal prayer; the other is a prayer of contemplation so high that our Lord shows himself in such a way as to make us feel he hears us.

Evening

Consoling me, our Lord told me once that I was not to distress myself – he said it most lovingly – because in this life we could not continue in the same state. At one time I might be fervent, at another not; now disquieted, and again at peace, and tempted; but I must hope in him and not be afraid.

I was one day wondering whether it was a lack of detachment in me to take pleasure in the company of those who had the care of my soul . . . Our Lord said to me: 'It is not a virtue in a sick man to abstain from thanking and loving the physician who seems to restore him to health.'

DAY

9

Morning

All I cared for then, as I do now, was that, as the enemies of God are so many and his friends so few, these latter might at least be good ones. Therefore I determined to do what little was in my power, which was to follow the evangelical counsels as perfectly as I could and to see that the few nuns here should do the same. Trusting in the great mercy of God which never fails those who resolve to leave all things for his sake, I hoped that, as my sisters here are all that I ever wished them to be . . . I might be able to bring some comfort to our Lord.

Evening

I will explain three matters only, which are in our Constitutions: it is essential for us to understand how much they help us to preserve that peace, both interior and exterior, which our Lord so strongly enjoined. The first of these is love for one another: the second detachment from all created things: the other is true humility, which, though I mention it last, is chief of all and includes the rest. The first matter, that is, fervent mutual charity, is most important, for there is no annoyance that cannot easily be borne by those who love one another.

DAY

10

Morning

Be cordial with your sisters when they take their needful recreation, and stay with them the whole of the appointed time, although it may not suit your taste . . . Make sure when it is right that you sympathize with and take pity on your sisters; you must always feel sorry for any conspicuous fault you see in one of them; charity is proved and tested in such a case by keeping patience and by not being shocked. Others bear in the same way with your faults, both those of which you are conscious and the many more of which you are ignorant.

Evening

The body possesses this defect – the more you give it, the more it requires. It is wonderful how fond it is of comfort, and what pretexts it will offer to obtain it, however little needed; it deceives the unfortunate soul and prevents its making progress. Remember how many poor people are ill and have no one to complain to – poverty and ease do not go together. Think, too, of the number of married women there are, many of them, as I know, of good position in life, who, lest they should annoy their husbands, dare not speak of the serious problems and poignant trials from which they suffer.

DAY

11

Morning

Interior mortification . . . is acquired little by little through never following our own will or desires even in the most trifling matters, until we have subdued the body to the spirit. I repeat that this is entirely or at least mainly accomplished by renouncing all care for ourselves and our own pleasure. If we have really begun to serve our Lord, the least we can offer him is our life, after having yielded our will to Him. What is there to fear in this? . . . Do you not know, sisters, that the life . . . of one who wishes to be among the most intimate friends of God is one long martyrdom?

Evening

If contemplation, mental and vocal prayer, nursing the sick, the work of the house and the most menial labour all serve this Guest who comes to eat and drink and converse with us, why should we choose to minister to him in one way rather than in another? Not that I mean that we have any choice as to the labours we shall perform, but you should practise them all, for the decision does not rest with you but with our Lord. But if, after many years' trial, he makes it clear what place each one is to fill, it would be a strange humility for you to choose for yourself. Leave that to the Master of the house: he is wise and powerful and knows what is best for you and for himself.

DAY
12

Morning

The soul understands that the divine Master is teaching it without the sound of words. He suspends the faculties, which by their action would hinder rather than favour contemplation. They are happy without knowing why: the soul is inflamed with love without comprehending how it loves: it feels that it enjoys the Beloved, yet how it does so it cannot tell. It realizes that this delight can never be gained through any desire of the mind itself: the will embraces its joy without apprehending how, yet it dimly perceives that every good work humankind could perform in this world would not merit such a reward, for it is the gift of the Lord of heaven and earth.

Evening

As you are alone, seek for some companion – and where could you find a better one than the Master who taught you the prayer you are about to say? Picture this same Lord close beside you. See how lovingly, how humbly he is teaching you – believe me, you should never be without so good a friend. If you accustom yourselves to keep him near you, and he sees that you love to have him and make every effort to please him, you will not be able to send him away. He will never fail you, but will help you in all your troubles and you will find him everywhere. Do you think it is a small thing to have such a friend at your side?

DAY
13

Morning

If you feel happy, think of him at his resurrection, for the very thought of how he rose from the tomb will delight you . . . If you have trials to bear, if you are sorrowful, watch him on his way to the garden . . . See him bound to the column, full of suffering, his flesh all torn to pieces . . . Or look on him again – laden with the cross . . . He will gaze at you with those beautiful, compassionate eyes, brimming with tears, and will forget his own grief to comfort yours, only because you went to comfort him and turned towards him.

Evening

Do not draw back from the cross nor abandon it. Often recall his weariness and how much harder his labours were than your own, however great you may fancy these to be and whatever pain they cause you. This will console you: you will go away comforted, seeing that they are but trifles compared with what our Lord bore . . .

Perhaps you will ask me, sisters, how you are to do this now, though if you had lived while Christ was on earth . . . you would willingly have done it . . . Do not believe this; if you will not use a little self-constraint now . . . much less would you have stood at the foot of the cross.

DAY

14

Morning

Those who are able thus to enclose themselves within the little heaven of their souls where dwells the Creator of both heaven and earth, and who can accustom themselves not to look at anything nor remain in any place that would preoccupy their exterior senses, may feel sure that they are travelling by an excellent way, and that they will certainly attain to drink of the water from the fountain, for they will journey far in a short time. They resemble a person who goes by sea and who, if the weather is favourable, gets in a few days to the end of a voyage that would have taken far longer by land.

Evening

In return for the short time spent in forcing ourselves to keep near [God], he will make us understand by certain signs that he is listening. Thus, if we have to recite the Pater Noster several times, he will show us that he heard us sufficiently the first time we said it, for he dearly loves to save us trouble. We need not repeat it more than once in a whole hour if we only apprehend that we are in his presence and know for what we are asking him, and believe that he is willing to grant it, like a tender father who loves to be with us and to enjoy our company.

DAY
15

Morning

The prayer of quiet . . . is a supernatural state to which no effort of our own can raise us, because here the soul rests in peace – or rather, our Lord gives it peace by his presence, as he did to the just man Simeon. Thus all the faculties are calmed, and in some manner, in no way connected with the exterior senses, the spirit realizes that it is close to its God, and that if it drew only a little nearer to him, it would become one with him by union. This is not because such a person sees him, either with physical eyes or spiritual sight. Nor did the just Simeon see anything more than the glorious but poor Infant . . . But the babe himself gave the old man light to recognize him.

Evening

The sublime perfection of this gospel prayer [the Our Father] is marvellous and we ought to thank God fervently for it. So admirably is it composed by the good Master that everybody may apply its meaning to their own wants. I am astonished at finding all perfection and contemplation enshrined in it, so that there seems to be no need to study any other writings. For here our Lord has taught us mental prayer from its very beginning, through the prayer of quiet and union up to the most high and perfect contemplation . . . If His Majesty sees that our works conform to our words, he will not fail to grant our prayers.

DAY

16

Morning

The illusions and temptations the devil plots against contemplatives are numerous. Such souls love fervently or they would not be contemplatives, and this is plainly shown in many ways, for a large fire throws a bright and clear flame. If they are wanting in love, let them be apprehensive and think they have good cause for fear: they should try to find out what is amiss and pray fervently. They must be very humble and must ask God not to lead them into temptation . . . But if they are lowly and try to find out the truth – if they submit to their confessor and are frank and outspoken with him, then – God is faithful.

Evening

I thought of the soul as resembling a castle, formed of a single diamond or a very transparent crystal, and containing many rooms, just as in heaven there are many mansions. If we reflect, sisters, we shall see that the soul of the just person is but a paradise, in which, God tells us, he takes his delight. What, do you imagine, must that dwelling be in which a King so mighty, so wise and so pure, containing in himself all good, can delight to rest? Nothing can be compared to the great beauty and capabilities of a soul; however keen our intellects may be, they are as unable to comprehend them as to comprehend God, for, as he has told us, he created us in his own image and likeness.

DAY

17

Morning

Now let us return to our beautiful and charming castle and discover how to enter it. This appears incongruous: if this castle is the soul, clearly no one can have to enter it, for it is the person himself: one might as well tell someone to go into a room he is already in! There are, however, very different ways of being in this castle; many souls live in the courtyard of the building where the sentinels stand, neither caring to enter farther, nor to know who dwells in that most delightful place, what is in it and what rooms it contains.

Certain books on prayer that you have read advise the soul to enter into itself, and this is what I mean.

Evening

In this part of the castle are found souls which have begun to practise prayer; they realize the importance of their not remaining in the first mansions, yet often lack determination to quit their present condition by avoiding occasions of sin, which is a very perilous state to be in.

However, it is a great grace that they should sometimes make good their escape from the vipers and poisonous creatures around them and should understand the need of avoiding them. In some ways these souls suffer a great deal more than those in the first mansions . . . as they begin to understand their peril.

DAY

18

Morning

These souls hear our Lord calling them, for as they approach nearer to where His Majesty dwells he proves a loving neighbour, though they may still be engaged in the amusements and business, the pleasures and vanities of this world. While in this state we continually fall into sin and rise again, for the creatures among whom we dwell are so venomous, so vicious and so dangerous that it is almost impossible to avoid being tripped up by them. Yet such are the pity and compassion of this Lord of ours, so desirous is he that we should seek him and enjoy his company, that in one way or another he never ceases calling us to him.

Evening

As for those who, by the mercy of God, have triumphed in these combats and persevered until they reached the third mansions, what can we say to them but 'Blessed is the one who fears the Lord'? . . . We may well call these souls blessed for, as far as we can tell, unless they turn back in their course they are on the safe road to salvation. Now, my sisters, you see how important it is for them to win their former battles, for I am convinced that our Lord will in future never fail to keep them in security of conscience, which is no small blessing.

DAY

19

Morning

A rich man, without son or heir, loses part of his property, but still has more than enough to keep himself and his household. If this misfortune grieves and disquiets him as though he were left to beg his bread, how can our Lord ask him to give up all things for his sake? This man will tell you he regrets losing his money because he wished to bestow it on the poor.

I believe His Majesty would prefer me to conform to his will and keep peace of soul while attending to my interests than worry about such charity as this.

Evening

Let us imagine we see two fountains with basins that fill with water . . . These two basins are filled in different ways: one with water from a distance flowing into it through many pipes and waterworks, while the other basin is built near the source of the spring itself and fills quite noiselessly. If the fountain is plentiful, like the one we speak of, after the basin is full the water overflows in a great stream which flows continuously. No machinery is needed here, nor does the water run through aqueducts.

DAY

20

Morning

Such is the difference between the two kinds of prayer. The water running through the aqueducts resembles appreciable devotion, which is obtained by meditation. We gain it by our thoughts, by meditating on created things, and by the labour of our minds; in short, it is the result of our endeavours, and so makes the commotion I spoke of, while profiting the soul. The other fountain, like divine consolations, receives the water from the source itself, which signifies God: as usual, when His Majesty wills to bestow on us any supernatural favours, we experience the greatest peace, calm and sweetness in the inmost depths of our being.

Evening

The silkworm symbolizes the soul which begins to live when, kindled by the Holy Spirit, it starts to use the ordinary aids given by God to all, and applies the remedies left by him in his Church, such as regular confession, religious books and sermons . . . Then it comes to life and continues nourishing itself on this food and on devout meditation until it has attained full vigour . . .

This shows, my daughters, how much, by God's grace, we can do, by preparing this home for ourselves, towards making him our dwelling-place as he is in the prayer of union.

DAY
21

Morning

As soon as, by means of this prayer, the soul has become entirely dead to the world, it comes forth like a lovely little white butterfly! . . .

It despises the work it did while yet a caterpillar – the slow weaving of its cocoon thread by thread – its wings have grown and it can fly; could it be content to crawl? All that it can do for God seems nothing to the soul compared with its desire. It no longer wonders at what the saints bore for him, knowing by experience how our Lord aids and transforms the soul until it no longer seems the same in character and appearance.

Evening

Souls seeking God's honour and glory more than their own are cured of the temptation . . . of thinking that human praise will cause them the injury they have seen it do to others. Nor do these souls care much about human contempt if, through them, anyone should praise God at least once . . .

These and other reasons to a certain extent allay the great distress formerly given by human praise, which, however, still causes some discomfort unless the soul has become utterly regardless of people's tongues. It is infinitely more grieved at being undeservedly esteemed by the world than by any slander; and when at last it becomes almost indifferent to praise, it cares still less for censure, which even pleases it and sounds like harmonious music to the ears.

DAY

22

Morning

Moses [was not] able to relate more than God willed of what he had seen in the burning bush; but unless the Almighty had clearly revealed certain mysteries to his soul, causing it to see and know its God was present, the lawgiver could never have undertaken so many and such great labours. The sublime revelations shown to him amid the thorns of the bush gave him the needful courage for his great deeds on behalf of the children of Israel. We must not, sisters, search out reasons for understanding the hidden things of God, but, believing him to be almighty, we should be convinced that such worms as ourselves . . . are unable to comprehend his wonders.

Evening

Neither the imagination nor the evil one could represent what leaves such peace, calm and good fruits in the soul, and particularly the following three graces of a very high order. The first of these is a perception of the greatness of God which becomes clearer to us as we witness more of it. Second, we gain self-knowledge and humility from seeing how creatures as base as ourselves in comparison with the Creator of such wonders have dared to offend him in the past or venture to gaze on him now.

The third grace is a contempt for all earthly things unless they are consecrated to the service of so great a God.

DAY

23

Morning

In the spiritual marriage with our Lord . . . the soul always remains in its centre with its God. Union may be symbolized by two wax candles, the tips of which touch each other so closely that there is but one light; or again, the wick, the wax and the light become one, but the one candle can again be separated from the other and the two candles remain distinct; or the wick may be withdrawn from the wax. But spiritual marriage is like rain falling from heaven into a river or stream, becoming one and the same liquid.

Evening

Perhaps when St Paul said, 'He who is joined to the Lord is one spirit,' he meant this sovereign marriage, which presupposes His Majesty's having been joined to the soul by union. The same apostle says: 'To me, to live is Christ and to die is gain.' This, I think, might here be uttered by the soul, for now the little butterfly of which I spoke dies with supreme joy, for Christ is her life.

This becomes more manifest by its effects as time goes on, for the soul learns that it is God who gives it 'life', by certain secret intuitions too strong to be misunderstood, and keenly felt, although impossible to describe.

DAY
24

Morning

Experience has shown me – setting aside what I have read in many places – what a great blessing it is for a soul never to withdraw from being under obedience. Herein lie, in my opinion, growth in goodness and the gaining of humility. Herein lies our security amid the doubts about whether or not we are straying from the heavenly road, doubts which, as human beings, it is right we should have while we are living here on earth. Herein is found that rest which is so dear to souls desirous of pleasing God; for, if they have really resigned themselves to holy obedience . . . Satan refrains from assailing them.

Evening

We had a well, the water in which was very bad according to those who tested it, out of which, because it was very deep, it seemed impossible to make the water flow. I sent for workmen to try and fix it; they laughed at me because I was going to throw money away. I said to my sisters, 'What do you think?' One of them answered, 'Let us try.' . . . Considering the great faith and resolution with which she said this, I took it for granted it would be so . . . Our Lord was pleased, and we have a flow of water, quite enough for us and good to drink, to this day.

DAY

25

Morning

O my Lord, when we see that you frequently deliver us from dangers into which we rush, even sometimes to offend you, how can anyone believe that you will not deliver us when our only aim is to please you, and in you to find our joy? . . . This, then, I am saying, should be a means to make us strive to travel on the road more diligently, that we may please the Bridegroom all the more and find him sooner, and not give up the attempt; it should encourage us to journey bravely on through the dangerous passes of this life.

Evening

It is very true that by meditating on the debt we owe our Lord, on his nature and on ours, a soul may attain a firm resolve – and there is great merit in doing so, and it is most fitting in the beginning; but it must be understood that what relates to obedience, and the good of our neighbour, to the doing of which charity constrains us, when either of these two is required of us, we must give up for the time that which we so much long to give to God; which, as we see it, is to be alone meditating upon him and rejoicing in his consolations. To give this up for either of the other two is to give pleasure to our Lord and do it for him.

DAY

26

Morning

[The man I spoke to] had been under obedience for fifteen years, charged with laborious offices and the government of others – so much so that he could not call to mind one day that he had had to himself; nevertheless he contrived to find, the best way he could, some time every day for prayer, and to have a clear conscience. He is one whose soul is the most given to obedience that I ever saw . . . Our Lord has amply rewarded him, for he finds himself, without knowing how, in possession of that freedom of spirit, so prized and so desired, that the perfect have, and wherein lies all the happiness that can be wished for in this life; for, seeking nothing, he possesses all things.

Evening

It is here, my children, that love must be made known; not in secret places, but in the midst of temptations: and trust me, our gain will be incomparably greater, though there may be more faults committed, and even some slight falls. Remember, in all I say I am taking for granted that you run these risks under obedience and out of charity, and if it not be so, my conclusion always is that to be alone is better; and, moreover, we ought to desire to be alone even when employed in the way I am speaking of; in truth, this desire is ever present in those souls that really love God.

DAY

27

Morning

O Lord, what a grand grace it is that you give those to whom you give such parents – parents who love their children so truly as to wish them to find their inherited self-respect, their position in life and their wealth in that blessedness that will never end! What a sad thing it is the world is so wretched and blind that fathers think their honour lies in preserving the memorials of their having been owners of the dunghills of this world's goods, and in the preservation of that which sooner or later must come to an end! And everything of which there is to be an end, however long it lasts, is perishing and deserves only scanty consideration.

Evening

His Majesty began to reward her immediately with spiritual graces, and she to serve him with the greatest joy, in the deepest humility and with detachment from all things. May he be blessed for ever who made the woman who had been once so fond of such rich and expensive garments take pleasure in the simple robe of serge! It could not, however, hide her beauty, for our Lord had given to her natural as well as spiritual graces; in her manners and her understanding she was so winning that she moved everybody to give God thanks for them. May His Majesty grant that there be many who answer like this to his call!

DAY

28

Morning

When I saw the little house, which just recently it was not possible to stay in, filled with such a spirit that, wherever I looked, there were things to inspire and uplift, and when I heard of their way of life, of their mortification and prayer, and of the good example they were giving . . . I could not thank our Lord enough in my exceedingly great joy, for I believed I was seeing a work begun that would greatly expand the order and increase the service of our Lord. May it please His Majesty to carry it on as it is going now so that what I thought I was seeing will become really true!

Evening

We continued to discuss the arrangements, and were looking for a house to let in order to take possession; none could be found fitted for the purpose, though diligent search was made, neither could I persuade the administrator to give us his permission . . . I did not know what to do, for I had come here for no other purpose but this . . . The refusal of the permission distressed me more than everything else, for I knew that, once in possession of a house, our Lord would provide, as he has done in other places; so I resolved to speak to the administrator . . . His heart was so touched that he gave me permission before I left him.

DAY
29

Morning

[The foundation at Salamanca] was the first foundation I made without the presence of the most holy sacrament, for I had not thought that I took possession if [our Lord] was not lodged in the house. I had now learnt that it made no difference, which was a great comfort to me, because the students had left the house in a very unseemly state, and, as they had but little regard for cleanliness, the whole place was in such a condition that we had no small work to do that night.

Early the next morning, Mass was said there for the first time, and I sent for more nuns . . . We shut ourselves up in a room where there was straw, that being the first thing I provided for the founding of the house, for with the straw we could not fail to have a bed.

Evening

The community remained in the same house for about three years . . . almost unheeded. But I was ordered to go to the monastery of the Incarnation in Avila, for of my own will I would never leave a house, nor did I leave any, till it was properly ordered and arranged, and here God has been very gracious to me. It is a joy to me to lead the work and I used to provide, even in the minutest details, whatever might be of use and comfort to the nuns, as if I had to live in that house all my life, and accordingly I was glad when the sisters were happily settled.

DAY

30

Morning

In that light she fixed her eyes on our Lord nailed to the cross shedding his blood, and thought of the ill treatment he received and of his great humility, and then how differently she was demeaning herself in her pride . . . He filled her with so great a desire to suffer for God that she wished she could undergo all the torments of the martyrs, giving her at the same time such an earnest longing for humiliation in her humility, with a loathing of self, that, if it had not been an offence against God, she could have wished herself one of the most abandoned of women . . . She made a vow of chastity and poverty on the spot.

Evening

[In order to refuse the proposed foundation] I must first speak to my confessor, the doctor Velasquez, canon and professor in Toledo, a most learned and excellent man, now bishop of Osma; for I am in the habit of never doing anything of my own will, but only at the will of persons such as he is. When he saw the letters and understood the matter he bade me not to refuse, but to answer kindly; for if God made so many hearts agree together on a thing it was plain he intended to be served thereby. I did so, for I neither accepted nor refused absolutely. Time went by as I was pressed and those who might persuade me were sought, until this year 1580; all the while I was thinking it folly to do so. When I made any reply I never could reply altogether unfavourably.

DAY 31

Morning

One day, still in doubt, and not decided on making either of the foundations, I implored our Lord, when I had just received communion, to give me light that I might in all things do his will: for my lukewarmness was not such as to make me falter for a moment in that desire. Our Lord said to me, as it were reproaching me, 'What are you afraid of? When did I ever fail you? I am today what I have always been; do not give up these two foundations.' O, great God, how different are your words from human words! So my courage and resolution came, the whole world was not strong enough to oppose me, and I began at once to make my preparations, and our Lord to provide the means.

Evening

I have always held that the nuns will never be in need because our Lord, who sends succour to monasteries dependent on alms, will raise up people to do much for this house, or will find means to maintain it . . . One day, thinking of this after communion, I heard our Lord say, 'Why doubt? This is now done; you may safely go' – giving me to understand that the nuns would never be in need of what might be necessary for them. I felt as if I were leaving them amply endowed, and have never been anxious about them since.

Notes and sources

Notes

1   Ruth Burrows, *Essence of Prayer* (Mahwah, NJ: HiddenSpring, 2006), p. 162.
2   Rowan Williams, *Teresa of Avila* (London: Continuum, 2003), p. 13.

Sources

Teresa of Avila, *The Autobiography of St. Teresa of Avila: The Life of St. Teresa of Jesus Written by Herself*, translated by David Lewis, re-edited with additional notes and introduction by Benedict Zimmerman (Charlotte, NC: Tan Books, 1997).

Teresa of Avila, *The Way of Perfection by St. Teresa of Avila*, translated by the Benedictines of Stanbrook, revised with notes and an introduction by Benedict Zimmerman (Charlotte, NC: Tan Books, 1997).

Teresa of Avila, *The Interior Castle*, translated by the Benedictines of Stanbrook, with an introduction by Benedict Zimmerman (Seattle, WA: Pacific Publishing Studio, 2011).

Teresa of Avila, *The Book of the Foundations of S. Teresa of Jesus*, translated by David Lewis, new and revised edition with introduction by Benedict Zimmerman (London: Thomas Baker, 1913).

The texts have been lightly modernized by Hannah Ward and Jennifer Wild.

Life
Day 1: Morning, 4.2–3; Evening, 7.1
Day 2: Morning, 10.4; Evening, 11.10
Day 3: Morning, 11.13; Evening, 13.3
Day 4: Morning, 14.1, 3; Evening, 15.5
Day 5: Morning, 16.1; Evening, 18.18
Day 6: Morning, 22.10; Evening, 24.6, 8
Day 7: Morning, 33.13, 14; Evening, 36.16, 17
Day 8: Morning, 39.8, 10; Evening, 40.23–4

Way
Day 9: Morning, 1.2; Evening, 4.3
Day 10: Morning, 7.6; Evening, 11.2
Day 11: Morning, 12.2; Evening, 17.5
Day 12: Morning, 25.1; Evening, 26.1
Day 13: Morning, 26.4; Evening, 26.6
Day 14: Morning, 28.5; Evening, 29.5

Day 15: Morning, 31.1; Evening, 37.1, 2
Day 16: Morning, 40.3

Castle
Day 16: Evening, 1.1.2
Day 17: Morning, 1.1.7–8; Evening, 2.1.2–3
Day 18: Morning, 2.1.4; Evening, 3.1.1
Day 19: Morning, 3.2.4–5; Evening, 4.2.3
Day 20: Morning, 4.2.4; Evening, 5.2.3, 4
Day 21: Morning, 5.2.6–7; Evening, 6.1.10, 11
Day 22: Morning, 6.4.7; Evening, 6.5.12–13
Day 23: Morning, 7.2.5; Evening, 7.2.6–7

Foundations
Day 24: Morning, Pr. 1; Evening, 1.3
Day 25: Morning, 4.4; Evening, 5.3
Day 26: Morning, 5.7; Evening, 5.16
Day 27: Morning, 10.9; Evening, 11.8
Day 28: Morning, 14.10; Evening, 15.5–6
Day 29: Morning, 19.3–4; Evening, 19.6
Day 30: Morning, 22.6; Evening, 28.9
Day 31: Morning, 29.6; Evening, 31.44